YOU

WHO ME?,

YES YOU

YOU

WHO ME?,

YES YOU

Pernell Stoney

XULON PRESS

Xulon Press
2301 Lucien Way #415
Maitland, FL 32751
407.339.4217
www.xulonpress.com

Unless otherwise indicated, Scripture quotations taken from the
King James Version (KJV) – *public domain.*

Printed in the United States of America.

ISBN-13: 978-1-54566-630-2

TABLE OF CONTENTS

ACKNOWLEDGMENTS

First, I give thanks and honor to my Lord and savior Jesus Christ, for it is through His blood that I am saved; to my wife Hwason, a true friend and woman of God, for loving me after 42 years through good and bad times. To my daughter Cherry, one of the sweetest people you could ever meet, who is always thinking of others first; and to my son, Steven, a man with strong values, who is always in my heart with a love that is unmatched. I would also like to thank my spiritual family: Pastor Johnny, Robin and Moses Williams, Pastor James, Gigi and DD Williams. We love you with the love of God. God has given all of you hearts of love and care. Thank you for being there for us.

Thanks to Dr. Michael and Benita Mitchell, my mentors and long-time friends of Restoration Ministries International (RMI) Christian Fellowship in Augusta Georgia, for teaching us the word of God. To Dr. Ron and Sue Rockwell, our pastors and spiritual leaders at Harvest Church in Phoenix, Arizona, thanks for being an example of not only teaching, but living a spiritually full life for the past seven years we were in Arizona. Thanks for teaching us how to love one another the way God wants us to. Special thanks to apostle John Evans for letting me know it was not my fault, but it was my time. Also, a very special thanks to our present pastors, Mirek and Linda Hufton of World Harvest Church in Roswell, Georgia, who boldly teach the Word of God, letting us know how to be true disciples, strong and bold in the Word of God. Thanks to Elder Willie and Flossie Russell for being strong leaders and mentors for all of us in the mission field.

Have a heart for others. To all of our family and friends, remember God loves you and so do we.

Again thanks,
Chreey

INTRODUCTION

You.

"Who me?"

Yes you.

As I look around watching and listening to what is being said. I concluded that you are living the world's way. It could be because you don't have knowledge of the power you could have as a man or woman of God. You are the center of attraction in this life, and the devil wants to take you out. He will show himself as an angel of light just to keep you confused, playing the blame game. You are always blaming someone for something you have control over, because you are looking through a one-way mirror. Seeing the fault of the other person and not looking at the part you played in that situation. Yes, you have a part in everything that concerns you. Remember that everything you know or learned came from someone or something. Guess what? You chose to do it or say it, so stop blaming others and accept your part in the situation. I pray that you will hear and receive what is being said throughout this book.

Chapter 1

MY TESTIMONY

For years I wrote love poems. Then, one evening in the spring of 2007, I was walking home from work thinking about the next poem I was going to write. I heard a small voice say, "tell your testimony, someone needs to know." I did not give it much thought at that time, but it stayed in my mind about telling my testimony. When I sat down to write, that small voice said, "now is the time." So I started writing. The title of the book became, *The Man I Should Be (The Reflection)*.

Over the years, I have accumulated many testimonies, but this one really answered many questions about angels watching over us. Now I see why God wanted me to tell my testimony. If my memory is correct, in 1986 my family and I took a trip to Cincinnati, Ohio to see my wife's sister. I was saved, or at least I thought I was, in my mind only. I was still smoking marijuana, getting high, and on the way to Ohio we pulled into a rest stop so I could rest for an hour. Instead of me resting, though, I pulled out a joint (weed) and started smoking. My wife and daughter were sleeping, so after smoking another joint I got back on the road. We were in a place called Loudon, Tennessee at that point.

About two hours back on the road I started feeling sleepy. Every once and awhile I would doze off, riding on the shoulder of the road. My wife woke up and ask me if I was ok. I said yes. I was not ok, and about thirty minutes later I fell asleep again, but this time I went too far off the road. I woke up in a panic mode, hitting the gas instead of the hitting the brakes. We hit a ditch at the speed we were going, causing the car to flip up and over, landing on the cab (top).

It landed on the other side of the interstate into oncoming traffic, sliding about 20 feet toward the oncoming traffic. The cab of the car was smashed, the front windshield was gone, the back glass was gone too. Looking out the back, I saw the headlights of something big coming toward us. The car was on a two-lane interstate highway, and our car was dead smack in the line of oncoming traffic. I believe my wife was praying in spirit. I don't know; all I knew was she was saying something, and I did not understand what she was saying. I was really worried about our daughter, who was in the back seat sleeping when all this happened. She did not have on a seatbelt when the car flipped, and my wife and I at the same time reached back to hold her down. The light we saw was a big 18-wheeler that stopped about 15 feet from us. The driver got out, ran over to the car and helped us out. He said he saw something on the road and slowed down once he got closer. He called 911, and when they came, they were all amazed that no one was hurt. At that time, I thanked God for protecting us. The car was a total loss, so it was a true miracle that we all were saved that early morning hour. I really knew then that God was real and He had angels watching over us.

This action was no one's fault but mine. I could blame the devil for me smoking marijuana, but he did not twist my arm nor put a gun to my head to make me smoke. No, it was ME. I had a choice—the wrong choice—and it nearly cost me and my family's lives. But to God be the glory. He saved us, and now I am a living testimony that he is alive. I will praise Him and let the world know His mercy endures forever. You can say I had my road to Damascus experience, like Paul, and now I am spreading the gospel to the world. God is real and we get to Him through his son Jesus.

Chapter 2

WHO IS IN CONTROL ON EARTH

With all that's going on in the world today, believers and non-believers are blaming God for EVERYTHING. I know everyone thinks God is in control, and yes, He is the creator of everything, and He can do what no man can do. We are free-willed humans. As you read this book, I pray the eyes of your understanding will be open to who's in control.

If you want to know who's in control on this earth, you must go back to the beginning to find out what happened. God created man and gave him (Adam) dominion over all the works of his hand; everything on this earth. Then Satan came on the scene and lied to Adam and Eve. When they disobeyed God and ate from the tree of good and evil, Adam gave up ownership of what God gave him. You can read the story in the book of Genesis 3:2-12 (Gen. 1:26, 27). The stage is set for the rest of this book.

People are blaming God for everything that is happening here on earth. And he is not the one to blame. I know your question is, "Then who is?" I am glad you asked. The Bible calls him Satan, the prince of this world. He has the lease, and God can't do anything about it. Satan is in control and God can't act on anything until he is asked to. Remember, God gave us free will to choose. He will not override you choosing to do what you want to do or situations you get into. We are always blaming someone else and not looking at ourselves. This is just my belief. I believe 100% of our problems are caused by us. Yes, you and me. Check this out:

> "There has no temptation taken you but such as is common to man [you]: but God is faithful, who will not suffer you to be tempted above that ye [you] are able; but will with the temptation also make a way to escape, that ye may be able to bear it" (1 Corinthians 10:13).

In other words, you will be tempted, but you will have to make the decision to get out of that temptation. God has already made a way for you to get out of it. So, stop waiting

on God to get you out of something you put yourself in.
Even though Satan is in control, God has set up a system
for you to overcome the fiery dots Satan is throwing at
you. I believe one of the major reasons we are caught in
Satan's devices is that we don't know who he is. We are in
a war, and this fight is in the spirit realm. We need to know
how and who we are fighting against and their capabilities.
Without knowing any of these things, we are fighting a war
blind, being led astray. During my readings and research,
I came across the following information. I pray this will
help you be more aware of the things you say and do and
who is to blame.

History of Satan – Where did he come from?

The history of Satan is described in the Bible in Isaiah
14:12-15 and Ezekiel 28:12-19 (KJV). These two biblical
passages also reference the king of Babylon, the King of
Tyre and the spiritual power behind the kings.

What caused Satan to be cast from Heaven? He fell
because of pride that originated from his desire to be God
instead of a servant of God. Satan was the highest of all
the angels, but he wasn't happy. He desired to be God

and rule the universe. God cast Satan out of heaven as a fallen angel.

History of Satan – Who is he?

Satan is often caricatured as a red-horned, trident-raising cartoon villain; no wonder people question the history of Satan. His existence, however, is not based on fantasy. It's verified in the same book that narrates Jesus' life and death (Genesis 3:1-16, Isaiah 14:12-15; Ezekiel 28:12-19; Matthew 4:1-11).

Christians believe Satan acts as the leader of the fallen angels. These demons, existing in the invisible spirit realm yet affecting our physical world, rebelled against God but are ultimately under His control. Satan masquerades as an "angel of light," deceiving humans just as he deceived Eve in the beginning (Genesis 3).

Jesus Himself testified of Satan's existence. During His ministry, He personally faced temptation from the devil (Matthew 4:1-11), cast out demons possessing people (Luke 8:27-33), and defeated the evil one and his legion of demon angels at the cross. Christ also helped us understand the ongoing, spiritual war between God and Satan, good and evil (Isaiah 14:12-15; Luke 10:17-20).

With Jesus Christ on our side, we need not fear Satan's limited power (Hebrew 2:14-15). We ought to be wise, however, in resisting his tactics:

"For though we live in the world, we don't wage war as the world does. The weapons we fight with are not the weapons of the world. On the contrary, they have divine power to demolish strongholds. We demolish arguments and every pretension that sets itself up against the knowledge of God, and we take captive every thought to make it obedient to Christ" (2 Corinthians 10:3-5).

History of Satan - What is his place now?

Throughout Satan's history, evil has been his identity, because he is directly opposite God's character. God's holy standard as found in the Bible exposes evil. If we do not rely on its truth, we can easily error by:

- Denying Satan's existence;
- Fearfully focusing on Satan rather than on Christ Jesus, who overcame him; and
- Outright worshiping Satan, preferring the darkness of evil rather than light that reveals sin (John 3:19; 2 Corinthians 11:14-15).

Any of these approaches please the devil. He wants us to deny, fear, obey or worship him. Unless we follow the trustworthy source, the Bible, Satan will deceive us (Ephesians 6:10-11).

History of Satan - Satan's seduction versus reality

In our scientific, rational age, spiritual beliefs are scorned as myth. Satan, however, doesn't mind those who rebuff the reality of fallen angels or demons. By masking himself, he can tempt and deceive people without blame. The wise will never forget that Satan and demons, determined to deceive humans, are fighting real battles and wars against heavenly angels.

Satan compels or entices his prey to follow him whether they realize it or not. Maybe they are simply ignorant and confused. Many would rather believe human theory than obey divine revelation and natural law. Whether blind, bound or brazenly willing, they join Satan for a doomed destiny. They condemn themselves to eternity in hell.

While Satan is more powerful than we humans, God doesn't leave us defenseless (Ephesians 6:10-11). At the Lord's rebuke, Satan and his demons shudder and flee (James 2:19; Jude 1:9). When Jesus Christ died, He overcame them (Colossians 2:15). Only in the authority of Jesus does anyone have power to stand against the devil. Those saved from sin by Jesus' death on the cross are protected; those who are not saved from Satan's power perish with him (John 3:16; 1 Peter 5:8-10).

I pray that this helped you understand who's in control of this world system. You also need to know that God has given you authority over the devil. You don't have to be like the devil, full of pride. If you look back at the things you did or are doing, pride is in it! Now the question is the pride that you are displaying: is it positive or is it negative? Always remember that you have full control of what you do or say. Yes, there are wicket spirits all around us, and we don't see them because they are in the spirit realm. These spirits influence you to say and do things. One of those things is to blame everyone else except yourself. We always have a choice no matter what situation or circumstance we may be in. God gave us that ability when his word said "choose you whom you will serve." What we need to do is accept Jesus as our Lord and Savior. Accepting Him, we must build a relationship with Him through reading his word, praising him and praying daily.

I gave you a description of the Devil so you'd know who you are fighting. Yes, we are fighting a fight that has already been won by our Lord and Savior Jesus Christ. If you have an enemy of war, then you need to learn all that you can about that enemy. How he looks, how he talks (communicates), how he acts and what type of weapons he uses. The battle we are fighting is in the spirit realm. We are fighting an enemy we can't see. Therefore, you need to know who you are up against. I pray the little I've given you will open the eyes of your understanding about who is in control of this world now. You need to take back what the Devil has stolen from you. You may be asking yourself, "What has he stolen from me?" Well, here are a few things from that long list.

a) **Joy**

b) **Peace**

c) **Love**

d) **Friendship**

e) **Faith (always doubting the word of God)**

f) **Truth (always lying deceiving other)**

g) **Communication with the Father**

h) **Kindness (full of hate for others)**

i) **Patience (not waiting on God)**

j) **Responsibility (not accepting things, blaming others)**

k) Hope (no desire to do the right thing)

l) Trust (not trusting in the word of God)

These are just a few things the Devil has taken from you and you don't realize it. Finally, my brothers and sisters, be aware of the 5 D's of the Devil.

1. **Disguise**: Satan has many ways of coming at YOU. If you are a person with an eye for the opposite sex or same sex and you are a married man or woman, he will disguise himself as the most beautiful male or female you have ever seen just to cause you to sin. If you are broke and need money, he will disguise a dishonest way to get the money, causing you to steal or even kill someone for the money. He is a master of disguise; I can go on and on about his disguises, but you get the picture. The word of God will bring those disguises to light.

2. **Distort**: He will try to confuse you by not letting you receive the correct information by bringing a multitude of things in your mind at the same time you are trying to hear or read the word of God. Confusion (gossip) is his game, and he knows that if he can keep you distorted and confused he can

recruit you into his army. So be wise to his tactics (1 Cor. 15:33).

3. **Divert**: His mission is to change your course to get you off the narrow road of eternal life. He wants you to get on the wide road of destruction (which so many of us are on at this very moment) that seems full of inequity (unfair or unjust) and sin. If it is not lining up with the word of God, it is a diversion of Satan. Let me give you an example of divert. It is payday and it is time to pay your tithes and give your offerings. There is a brand new cell phone that just came out and you having been waiting for some time. The more you think about the phone the easier it is for Satan to divert you from paying your tithes and giving your offerings. He will tell you that you can make it up the next paycheck. This is how he operates; he will help you bring that thought into reality. One way you will know it is a diversion of the devil is to know the word of God.

4. **Deny**: He will try to get you to believe the word of God is untrue, just as he did Eve in the garden. You can read the story in the book of Genesis Chapter 3. He will harden your heart, and you will refuse to believe the word of God. The word tells us that

God's people are destroyed for the lack of knowledge and the rejection of knowledge (Hosea 4:6). When you study the word (2 Tim 2:15) you can overcome the tricks of the devil.

5. **Discredit**: He will destroy your reputation with lies and disbelief, he will start rumors and he will cause you to lose trust in what God can and will do for you. He will whisper anything in your ears to make you think you are hearing in a spiritual manner. He'll cause you to act out in the flesh, hurting the ones you love. That is why it is so important to put on the Armor of God (Eph. 6:10-18).

Remember his primary mission here on earth is steal, kill, and destroy you. This battle is taking place in the spirit realm, creating physical acts of disobedience in the flesh (Eph. 6:12). With this being said, we need to go to the firing range (the word of God) daily to protect our kill shot (fiery dots).

**Remember this is all about you and
what you do or don't do.**

Chapter 3

WHO IS GOD?

Now I will tell you about our Creator of the world, and what He has given us to fight this spiritual battle and win. You must know who always has your back when things are going great and when things are not going so great. In times of trouble, who can you call on? Most people don't know who God is. Well, the Bible *tells* you who he is. So please read the Bible and ask God for understand of things you don't understand. Remember Hosea 4:6. If you don't know it, I suggest that you read it.

God is the creator of all things, and He created all things for His pleasure. After the sixth day of creation, Moses records God's thoughts as: "And God saw everything that he had made, and, behold, it was very good. And the evening and the morning were the sixth day" (Genesis 1:31). In heaven, the twenty-four elders say, "Thou art worthy, O Lord, to receive glory and honor and power: for

Thou hast created all things, and for Thy pleasure they are and were created" (Revelation 4:11).

And speaking of Christ as part of the Godhead, the apostle Paul writes, "For by Him were all things created, that are in heaven, and that are in earth, visible and invisible, whether they be thrones, or dominions, or principalities, or powers: all things were created by Him, and for Him: And He is before all things, and by Him all things consist" (Colossians 1:16–17). John tells us, "In the beginning was the Word, and the Word was with God, and the Word was God. The same was in the beginning with God. All things were made by Him; and without Him was not anything made that was made" (John 1:1–3). Clearly our God is an omnipotent God. He is the ultimate one who controls things. But he will not break the contract that Adam gave to Satan in the Garden of Eden. He also gave all of us a mind of our own to make decisions for ourselves. He will not go against what we choose to do. He may not agree with the choices you make, but just remember it is you that is making them. It is not God that is creating the negative things in your life, it is you and the decisions you are making. In the book of John 10:10 it reads, "The thief [Satan] cometh not, but for to steal, and to kill, and to destroy: I [Jesus] am come that they [you and me] might have life, and that they might have it more abundantly."

As you can see, God wants you to have an abundant life, so stop blaming him for all the negative things that are happening in your life. Get instruction on how to live an abundant life., He has given you all the help you need to live the way he wants you to live. If you put Him first you will never be last in anything you do!!!

Trinity

During my study and research, below is what I found on the Trinity.

Have you ever wondered about the doctrine of the Trinity? How could the God of the Bible be one God, but at the same time three persons—Father, Son, and Holy Spirit? Doesn't the Bible emphatically state that God is one? These queries are common discussions among Christians and non-Christians alike.

The Bible should be accepted as the final authority for the believer. Therefore, we must look to scripture to learn what God has revealed about Himself in His inspired Word. The famous passage known as the Shema (Hebrew: "hear") starts by stating, "Hear, O Israel: The LORD our

God, the LORD is one! You shall love the LORD your God with all your heart, with all your soul, and with all your strength" (Deuteronomy 6:4–5).

The Bible is quite clear: God is one!

The Bible is also clear that there are three persons who are each called God. This plurality of God is presented in 2 Corinthians 13:14: "The grace of the Lord Jesus Christ [the Son], and the love of God [the Father], and the communion of the Holy Spirit [the Holy Spirit] be with you all. Amen." With our finite minds, it is impossible to fully comprehend the infinite God. It is also difficult for us to comprehend the concept that God is one being in three persons.

The Trinity in Isaiah

The prophet Isaiah made a statement that supports the doctrine of the Trinity:

> "Come near to Me, hear this: I have not spoken in secret from the beginning; from the time that it was, I was there. And now the Lord GOD [the Father] and His Spirit [the Holy Spirit] have sent Me [the Son].

> Thus, says the LORD, your Redeemer, the
> Holy One of Israel: I am the LORD your God,
> who teaches you to profit." (Isaiah 48:16–17)

All three persons of the Trinity are explicitly mentioned in this passage.

Conclusion

The Bible is quite clear—there is one true God, and He exists in three persons: God the Father, God the Son, and God the Holy Spirit. There is salvation in no other God. This Trinitarian God is eternal, as stated in Isaiah. God the Father, in the power of God the Holy Spirit, through the agency of God the Son—Jesus Christ—created everything that exists. John 1, Colossians 1 and Hebrews 1 all teach that the Lord Jesus is the Creator. Since He is our Creator, He has the right and the authority to be our Redeemer. Jesus said, "I am the way, the truth, and the life. No one comes to the Father except through Me. If you had known Me, you would have known My Father also; and from now on you know Him and have seen Him" (John 14:6–7).

The doctrine of the Trinity is not derived from pagan beliefs, but was developed from the plain teachings of scripture. God is one being in three persons. Answers in Genesis provide numerous passages concerning the various attributes and works of each member of the Trinity.

I've added all this to let you know that God created all of what you see and what you don't see, meaning the good spirits that are in heavenly places. Some have turned evil (the devil) and are causing all this mess that is happening on this earth today. Make no mistake, the earth and all that is in it belong to God. He has set in place everything we need to overcome any situation we may get in. That tells me you are the reason for your current situation. There is no situation that is faultless, so stop blaming other people for what you could do or could not do. Look in the mirror and you will see the answer to your situation. We must read the Basic Instruction Before Leaving Earth (BIBLE).

One of our greatest setbacks is our lack of spiritual knowledge. "My people are destroyed for lack of knowledge, because thou hast rejected knowledge" (Hosea 4:6). What you need has been provided for you to make it in this world and to heaven. God is not going to do anything else until you learn of Him and activate the power and the authority he has given you.

Questions

Can you answer the following questions? If you can, write who will you turn to, and why you will turn to them.

1. Are you broken?_____
   a. How does this brokenness affect your relationship with God? _____
2. Is it possible for God to put the broken pieces of your life back together? _____
   a. Why is it possible? _____
3. What changes take place when you become a follower of Christ? _____
   a. How do these changes affect every aspect of your life? _____
   b. Who will make the changes? _____
   c. What do I need to do to make the changes? _
4. What is the authority I have? _____
   a. Where does this authority come from? _____
   b. How much authority does Satan have over me and why?_____
5. How can I activate the power that was given to me?_____
6. Who controls what I do and say and why? _____

7. Who am I? _____

8. What does the bible say about me? _____

9. Who is the center of attraction of this world and why? _____

10. What is faith and where does it come from? _____

Extra Reading

Romans 10:17

Chapter 4

MERCY, GRACE AND FAITH

I think these need to be explained so you can understand them a little more. All of us have mixed these up in the past, all because we don't know the meaning of them. I hope the following will give you a better understanding of the differences between mercy, grace and faith.

What are mercy and grace?

Mercy and grace are often confused. While the terms have similar meanings, grace and mercy are not the same. To summarize the differences:

Mercy is God not punishing us as our sins deserve it. **Grace** is God blessing us even though we do not deserve it. **Mercy** is deliverance from judgment. **Grace** is extending kindness to the unworthy.

According to the Bible, you have sinned (Ecclesiastes 7:20; Romans 3:23; 1 John 1:8). As a result of that sin, you deserve death (Romans 6:23) and eternal judgment in the lake of fire (Revelation 20:12-15). With that in mind, every day you live is an act of God's mercy. If God gave us all of what we deserved, then we would all be condemned for eternity. In Psalms 51:1-2, David cries out, "Have mercy on me, O God, according to thy lovingkindness: according unto the multitude of thy tender mercies blot out my transgressions. 2. Wash me thoroughly from mine iniquity, and cleanse me from my sin."

A plea to God for mercy is asking Him to withhold the judgment we deserve and instead grant to us the forgiveness we in no way have earned. We *deserve* nothing from God. God does not *owe* us anything. Anything good that we experience is a result of the grace of God (Ephesians 2:5). Grace is simply defined as unmerited favor. God's favor gives you good things that you do not deserve and could never earn. Rescued from judgment by God's mercy, grace is anything and everything we receive beyond that mercy (Romans 3:24). Common grace refers to the sovereign grace which God bestows on all of mankind regardless of their spiritual standing before Him, while saving grace is that special dispensation of grace whereby God sovereignly bestows unmerited divine assistance upon His elect for their regeneration and sanctification.

Mercy and grace are best illustrated in the salvation that is available through Jesus Christ. We deserve judgment, but if we receive Jesus Christ as Savior, we receive mercy from God and we are delivered from judgment. Instead of judgment, we receive by grace salvation, forgiveness of sins, abundant life (John 10:10), and an eternity in Heaven, the most wonderful place imaginable (Revelation 21-22). Because of the mercy and grace of God, our response should be to fall on our knees in worship and thanksgiving. Hebrews 4:16 declares, "Let us then approach the throne of grace with confidence, so that we may receive mercy and find grace to help us in our time of need."

Chapter 5

YOU

You are the most important of all God's creations. You were created in His image, and that image is His spirit, not the fleshly body. The reason you have this fleshly body is because you need it for the world we live in. Don't forget you were created for His glory. "Everyone that is called by my name: for I have created him for my glory. I have formed him; yea, I have made him" (Isaiah 43:7 KJV). You can also read Revelation 4:11. We are to give honor and glory to God. You may ask "How do I do that?" Well, I am glad you asked. You must follow the instructions in the Bible. For you to do that, you must have faith and believe. For you to believe something, you must have faith in it. His word is no different. Psalms 37:4 tells us "Delight thyself [you] also in the LORD; and He shall give thee [you] the desires of thine [your] heart."

The word of God was written for you, that you may receive all that he has for you. Here are a few things that are stopping you from receiving the power God has given to resist the devil and not fall for his tricks. You must be aware of what you are saying and doing.

1. **Relationships**: You must build a relationship with Him (Jesus). You do that by reading/ studying the Bible and praying daily.

2. **Faith**: Have faith when hearing the word of God, listen to the men of God who are teaching the Bible. If what they are saying is not lining up with God's word, then don't retain it. The word tells us there are false prophets and teachers. It tells us of the danger of false teachers, the destruction of false teachers and the description of false teachers. Therefore, it so important to read the word of God. After reading II Peter 2: 1-21, you don't have any reason to not have faith.

3. **Blame**: You are being insecure in yourself, always blaming others.

4. **Fear**: Being fearful of everything and everybody, when the word of God tells you he has not given you the spirit of fear, but of power and of love and

of a sound mind (2 Timothy 1:7 KJV). That fear that you have is of the devil and not of God. Everybody can be fearless, if they accept Jesus Christ as their Lord and Savior.

5. **Prayer**: Your prayer life is hit and miss. You pray only when you need something from the Father. Most of the time we don't even do that right! We go straight to the Father and not through Jesus Christ, which the word tell us if we want anything from the Father we must ask for it in the name of Jesus.

6. **Worship**: You don't worship. You may not go to church or if you do go to church you just stand or sit and say nothing while everyone else is worshipping and praising God. "God is a Spirit: and they that worship him must worship him in spirit and in truth" (John 4:24). "But the hour cometh, and now is, when the true worshippers shall worship the Father is spirit and truth: for the Father seeketh such to worship him" (John 4:23 KJV).

Satan wants you to be like five of the ten virgins. If you don't know the story, I will tell you about them, and you can also read about them in Matthew 25. There were ten virgins, all of whom knew the bridegroom (Jesus Christ)

28

was coming. They needed to be ready when he came, so they took their lamps and went to meet him. Five of them were wise, and five were foolish. They who were foolish took no oil with them (they were not ready and they let the things of the world keep them from being ready, saying to themselves they had time). But the wise (5) took oil within their vessels with the lamps. They were obedient to the words of the bridegroom; they were ready to meet him. While the bridegroom tarried (to linger, delay), they all fell asleep. And at midnight there was a cry made, "behold the bridegroom cometh; go ye to meet him. Then all the virgins arose and trimmed [to put in order, arrange, make ready, prepare] their lamps. The foolish said unto the wise, give us some of your oil for our lamps for they are going out." The wise answered no, we are not giving you any of our oil. "But go ye rather to them that sell, and buy for yourself. While they went to buy, the bridegroom came; and they that were ready went in with him to the marriage: and the door was shut." Afterward came the 5 foolish virgins who had gone to get oil for their lamps, saying, "Lord, Lord, open to us, but he answered and said, verily I say unto you, I know you not. This is what he told them, watch therefore, for [you] know neither the day nor hour wherein the Son of man cometh."

I believe we are living out the story of the ten virgins. I advise to not be like the five foolish virgins. True believers of Christ have faith, are obedient to his word, rebuke the gods of this world, fight the good fight and stand their ground. These are the wise that are keeping oil in their lamps and extra to refill it. The foolish are the ones that are disobedient to the word, playing church and letting the cares of this world keep them in bondage, putting everything before God. Putting your faith in what you have or don't have. The Holy Spirit tells you to pay your tithes, and the spirit of the devil tells you that the cell phone you want is on sale and you can certainly use the fifty dollars from your tithes.

It doesn't have to be a cell phone. It could be anything that you have been admiring. The devil knows when you begin to admire something and will place the desire in your heart. Once you have the desire in your heart, now you will acquire it. Anything that goes against what you are doing for the kingdom of God, the devil will place that negative thought of things in your heart. So, don't be like the five foolish virgins. Be ready always. You must make a daily deposit into your spiritual account. You may ask "What am I putting in this account?" I believe the following are just a few things you can deposit: worship, prayer, study, compassion for others. Remember no good deed goes unrewarded.

We must live out the word as best as we can, keeping our spiritual account updated and overflowing. God is on your side. Remember faith without works is dead. Read James 2:20.

> "For as the body without the spirit is
> dead, so faith without works is dead also."
> (James 2:26)

Words are very powerful, they can make you or break you. Our destination is determined by the words we speak, and it does not matter if they are positive or negative. They dictate our journey. What I am telling you is you are the one that controls your life. All you must do is follow the instruction that was given to you.

If you want to know why you are not moving forward in life, listen to what you are saying. Turn to Prov. 21:23 "Whoso ever keepeth his mouth and his tongue keepeth his soul from troubles."

Here are a nineteen things to think about that are very common to man. These things are spoken daily, and they are stopping us from receiving our blessings. When we are not saying them, we are blaming someone else for our lack of knowledge.

You Say	God Says	Bible Verses
1. It's impossible:	All things are possible.	(Luke 18:27)
2. I am so tired:	I will give you rest.	(Matt: 11:28-30)
3. Nobody loves me:	I love you.	(John 3:16 & 3:34)
4. I can't go on:	My grace is sufficient.	(II Cor. 12:9/Ps.91:15)
5. I can't figure things out:	I will direct your steps.	(Psalms 3:5-6)
6. I can't do it:	You can do all things.	(Philippians 4:13)
7. I am not able:	I am able.	(II cor. 9:8)
8. It's not worth it:	It will be worth it.	(Roman 8:28)
9. I can't forgive myself:	I forgive you.	(I John 1:9 Rom8:1)
10. I can't manage:	I will supply all your needs.	(Philippians 4:19)
11. I'm afraid:	I have not given you the spirit of fear.	(II Tim1:7)

12. I am always worried and frustrated:	Cast all your cares on Me.	(1Peter 5:7)
13. I am not smart enough:	I give you wisdom.	(1 Cor. 1:30)
14. I feel all alone:	I will never leave you or forsake you.	(Hebrews 13:5)
15. I don't have anything:	Ask and you shall receive.	(John 16:24/ Psalms 37:4-5)
16. I can't trust anyone:	Put your trust in me said the Lord.	(Psalms 4:5)
17. I don't understand:	Through faith we understand.	(Heb. 11:3)
18. I don't have the strength:	Calleth those things which be not as though they were.	(Roman 4:17). You are not being positive enough in your daily walk with the Godhead Father, Son and Holy Spirit.
19. I can't for-give them:	Forgive; and, ye shall be forgiven.	(Luke 6:37).

There are many more things we say and do that do not line up with the word of God. Therefore, Satan gets the best of YOU. Remember the words you speak will determined the action you take. You are not perfect and God is not looking for a perfect person, he is looking for willing souls. Someone that is obedient to his word.

As a Christian or not you are an open book. But when you say you are a Christian you are read very closely and in detail by everyone. Even the ones that are not saved will tell you how you should act and what to say. Why is this? Well, you claim to be a Christian and everyone expects you to live a perfect life. It is impossible to live a perfect life, but you should live according to the word of God. Your words and your actions will do one of two things: 1) draw men into the kingdom, or 2) turn them away. The question I have for you, is which one are you doing? As I stated before, you are the centerpiece of everything around you. God created you to be the centerpiece of things on this earth. Look around you, everyone is making a statement, and I mean everyone. You may say "who me?" and I would say "yes you." Here are some of the ways statements are made.

1. The things we say, when we should not say them.
2. The things we do, when we should not do them.
3. The clothes we wear, when we should not wear them.
4. The things we don't do, the things we should do.

5. The things we don't say, the things we should say.

These five things tell people who you are. As I stated before, you are an open book. You are being read every day, so the question is what do you want people to read about you. You want to be a man or woman with honor, praising and worshipping God daily. If you want to make a change in your life, you must stop doing what you are doing for the change to start. Remember you are in control of your life and not Satan. He only has power over you because you give it to him. You must know how to resist the devil. In the book of James 4:7 tells us: "Submit yourselves therefore to God. Resist the devil, and he will flee from you."

Chapter 6

YOUR CHILDREN

This is a very hot subject, and I am going to tell you what the Bible says about our children. After this, you can stop blaming others for your neglect or your disobedience. The book of Deuteronomy 6:6, 7 says the following:

> "And thou shalt love the Lord thy God with all thine heart, and with all thy soul, and with all thy might. And these words, which command thee this day, shall be in thine heart. And thou shalt teach them diligently unto thy children, and shalt talk of them when thou sittest in thine house, and thou walkest by the way, and when thou liest down, and when thy risest up." (Deuteronomy 6:5-7)

"Train up a child in the way he should go:
and when he is old, he will not depart from
it." (Proverbs 22:6)

My question is are you doing what the word of God
said? I don't believe we are because of what is happening
to our children today. We are letting social media and bad
associations raise them. What they are not learning on
social media, we are teaching them. Let me give you a few
examples of what we are teaching them:

1. You talk about people in front of your children. You
   say bad things about the pastor and his wife, riding
   in the car coming from church and at home.
2. You disrespect each other by calling each other
   names in front of your children, and you expect
   them to respect you and others.
3. You say all kind of vile things around them.
4. You watch all kinds of sin-provoking movies
   with them.
5. You let them stay out late at night.
6. You let them smoke and drink at an early age.
7. You let them read/watch pornography magazines
   and movies.

8. You let them dress any kind of way.

9. You neglect your duties as parents, disobedient to God's word, and when the children become unruly, we can't do anything with them. Now, we put the blame on others when they do wrong or when someone tries to correct them.

Now that they've grown up so fast, we are trying to discipline them. We have allowed them to be raised by the world, and now we don't have control or influence over them. They say what they want, they do what they want, they dress the way they want, and they have no respect for others. When they dress or say certain things, they are just being kids. Well, these kids are killing each other, and adults are also being killed. You ask yourself, where did all this come from or when did this start? This is what I believe. After reading Deuteronomy 6:5-7 and Hosea 4:6, this is why we are in the mess we are in today with our youth.

*Note to the Children: If you are reading this book, it is not too late for you to accept Jesus Christ as your Lord and Savior. Repeat the following words out loud from the bottom of your heart. Why the heart? Because God looks at the heart (Luke 6:45, Matthew 15:18). Please repeat these words:

Father, in the name of Jesus I ask for forgiveness. I repent of my sin and I ask you to come into my life. Give me the wisdom and knowledge of your word that I may be bold and strong in you. In the name of Jesus, I pray.

Now that you have said this prayer, you must begin changing your ways. You must start by reading the Bible, which the church teaches as the true word of God. Begin reading your Bible daily (if you don't have one, purchase one or download it off the internet—they are free). Also, begin praying every day and night. The more you communicate with God, the more He will communicate with you. Remember, you are the seeds of tomorrow. We can't lose any more ground. We must take back what the devil has taken.

As a child, you must honor your parents because the word of God tells you to. Most people will say to respect them. Always remember that everything we know and do is a learned response from somebody or something.

Chapter 7

DANIEL

This chapter is the testimony of a young man name Daniel F. His testimony is so powerful I had to ask him if could I put it in this book. I believe what he says about himself touches all of us in some way. In this world of technology, we have forgotten our first love, which is Jesus Christ. You wake up on your phone, you go to bed on your phone, desktop, laptop or TV. You have put the Bible on the top shelf. If this is happening, then your prayer life is also on the shelf. It is all you.

"Who me?" Yes you.

Daniel F.

I grew up in the church from birth. I had seen and heard countless sermons, countless services, countless testimonies, you name it. With my own eyes, I had seen God do mighty things in people's lives, many, many times. I'd been through revivals and youth camps, mission trips and outreaches, year, after year, after year.

Despite all of this, and despite everything I had been exposed to on a regular basis, my life was anything but Godly. I had no self-control and no self-discipline. I had high academic expectations for myself and great poten-tial, and yet I would procrastinate to no end, spend all my time in gaming and media, run from work and stress, skip school, and after it all, I would hate myself for it. I con-stantly dealt with depression. I knew what I needed to do and why I needed to do it, but I couldn't make myself. I was in complete bondage. My life at home was a living nightmare, as was my relationship with my parents. When I cried out to God, nothing seemed to change. It didn't seem like He was there.

However, God did not abandon me. By His mercy, I barely managed to graduate in four years and make it out on the other side. My relationship with my parents had been getting better, and I was free from the depression I had suffered with earlier on in high school. Around three months later, at 18 years old, in the fall of 2017, I had taken a semester off before my first year of college and wasn't employed; I had lots of free time and not many

responsibilities to worry about. God had fixed everything, right?

Nope. I still struggled with the same sin, the same habits
and the same lifestyle that I had hated before. I was still
the same person, and deep down I still had no idea what
it meant to have a real relationship with God. Those past
experiences I had so recently overcome always lurked in
the back of my mind, and I was, in truth, very fearful that
as soon as I got started with college and had more responsibilities to deal with, all those things that had destroyed
me before would come flooding back in and overtake me.
God's presence in my life was still as shallow as it was
before. Why doesn't God speak to me? Why doesn't God
touch me? Why doesn't God change me?

What's wrong with me? Why can't I stop sinning? Why
am I so lazy? Am I even truly saved? These are the questions I had struggled with my entire life, and they were
still as present as they ever were.

What happened next? Well, it was in December of
2017, a month before I was going to start school. My entire
life was shaken and transformed, from the inside-out. In a
single month, I saw more of God's work in me and more
change in me than I had ever seen my entire life. Suddenly,
I knew beyond a shadow of a doubt that I was saved.

Suddenly, I had *victory* in my life. I had *victory* over sin. I had *victory* over my bad habits. My motivations began to change. My heart began to change.

I could tell you how it all happened and all the wonderful things that God did, but, first, what is truly important and completely *essential* is where it all began.

I got real with myself. I got tired of the struggle and of all the confusion, and I realized that I didn't know God at all. I got tired of doing the same thing over, and over, and over again. It started with one, small goal: to read and understand the Gospels, from scratch. I didn't even use any kind of daily Bible plan or schedule, and I ignored everything I originally thought I knew or understood about God. I came before God in complete humility, admitting that I was completely blind, lost, and confused and needed him to change me. You see, we can cry out to God all we want Him to speak to us and guide us, but His word is already at our fingertips. If we truly wanted Him, we would read it. I, to this day, am the most irresponsible and lazy person I have ever known, but that month I not only read Bible every day, but I also read the New Testament from start to finish. If you read the Bible, for content and understanding, in humility and in faith, putting your trust in God for the change and confessing to him that you are a blind and helpless sinner without him, he will come through mightily. I *implore* you. Just start with a small goal.

Read the Gospels and understand them. Open your heart and abandon your pride before a God who loves you infinitely, yearning earnestly in every passing moment for you to turn to him. See what happens.

Now, I'm going to share perhaps the most important aspect of what has changed in my life. **First, let me start with this:** I live in a first world country, in a middle class family. I hardly had to ever worry about whether I was going to have food to eat or clothes to wear or whether I was going to be sleeping in the rain. As for teenagers who don't have it as well as I did, even they don't really worry much about those things either.

No, what we're worrying about is that new hit show on Netflix. We like to binge-watch for hours, and we're very familiar with the emptiness that's left after we finish that last episode and the excitement dies down. We get so hyped about that next gaming console generation and that next big game, wasting away hours of our life in the entertainment. We're so concerned with how many likes we got and how many followers we have, so concerned with "Did they reply to my snap? Did they watch my story?" getting our approval from other people. We love to scroll and surf through memes and YouTube videos endlessly, pointlessly, drowning in entertainment. We worry so much about that guy, about that girl, and we want someone to validate us, someone we can be intimate with. We seek fruitlessly for pleasure, satisfaction, and validation.

Jesus said, "But woe to you who are rich, for you have received your consolation. Woe to you who are full, for you shall hunger. Woe to you who laugh now, for you shall mourn and weep. Woe to you when all men speak well of you, for so did their fathers to the false prophets" (Luke 6:24-26). Nothing in this world can ever fill the void in our souls. Though we may have our physical needs met, only Jesus can meet the spiritual needs every person has at the core of their very being.

Everything else is just a substitute, an idol. Yes, idol worship is rampant in our culture today! Unless we turn to God and away from our worldly pleasures to meet those needs, to satisfy us and fill us, to give us joy and happiness, we will always be empty, and we lie to God's face when we say that we are hungry for him and for his presence. Personally, I had to give up video games completely. I also had to cut off media and entertainment, having no plan for when I would allow them back in. I obeyed God, in faith, knowing it was not by my own strength or holiness, and everything changed. It *began* with reading the Gospels, but *that* is where it got real. That's where the victory started. I was no longer bound by that need for entertainment, and now there was finally room in my heart for God to come in and do his work.

Chapter 8

PARENTS/ADULTS

"Who me?" Yes you.

As parents we were given the responsibility to teach, raise up our children in the way they should go (Deuteronomy 6:5-7). But you are not, you are letting everyone else raise/teach them. You are conforming to the things of this world and not the word of God. You want to dress like them (your children), men/fathers wearing your clothes hanging off your butt. Women/mothers wearing jeans with holes all in them, places where holes should not be, chest hanging out, skirts above the knee trying to look young and act young. Please don't misunderstand—there is nothing wrong with looking young. But trying to act young is something different. You should be acting in the manner that reflects your age, being honored in the way you carry yourself and wearing clothes in a modest style. When people speak about how you dress or stare at you, don't blame them. You created the conversation of people around you. You want to talk like them, you want to act like them, you let them dishonor you, all because you want to be their friend instead of being their parents. They look at a friend in a different way than you.

When you are not obedient to the word of God, you lose sight of things and begin to blame everyone else for what you did or what you did not do. There is no curfew in the home they come and go as they please. We have created a generation that is always denying the truth and blaming others. They talk back to you, and you say they are just being teenagers. You are waiting on others to validate you in what you are or are not doing. Then we blame them if things are not going right or the way you want it to go. You have the Basic Instruction Before Leaving this Earth (Bible), but you are not following the instructions. Now who is to blame? This book is written in hope of helping you understand the things that are happening to you all because of you.

"Who me?" Yes you and no one else.

This is not what God had planned for you when he died for our sins. He left specific instructions for us to follow. The devil has no tempting power over you unless you give it to him. This is what you have done. You may be saying, "How do I know this?" I am glad you asked. My answer is to look around you or even in the mirror. This is what the word of God tells us. "There hath no temptation taken you, but such as is common to man: but God is faithful, who will not suffer you to be tempted above that ye are able; but will with the temptation also make a way to escape, that ye may be able to bear it" (1 Corinthian 10:13). What this tells me is I have a choice in everything that happens to me. You are the one to blame for the things that happen to you.

"Who me?" Yes you.

Jesus died on the cross and defeated the devil, all because he loves you. He did not blame us for our sinful lives, and he gave you a way out. You are the one who controls your life, so stop blaming others for everything that does not go your way. No, you are not perfect, but God is not looking for perfect people. He is looking for obedient and compassionate souls. Remember, we were created in his image (Gen 1:27). What I am telling you is not hearsay; I am speaking from experience. As a parent myself I have been there, I have done some of the things you are doing or have done, and I may have done some things you may not have done. The past 15 years my life has really changed. In 2017, the spirit opened the eyes of my understanding, showing me the "you" factor, which includes me. It was like my life flashed before me, where I was blaming others for my failures and shortfalls in life. I was in the center of all of it, not knowing I made the choice to be in whatever situation I was in.

"All power is given unto me in heaven and
in earth." (Matthew 28:18)

Also read: Eph. 6:12 (Eph. 1:22) (Exo. 14:14) (1 John 4:4) (Colossians 2:13-15) (Psalms. 118:22)

The devil has no power over Jesus; he has no power over you. But if you don't know, the devil has been defeated, the devil will take advantage of you. When Jesus defeated the devil, we also have victory over the devil. When Jesus died on the cross, we also died on the cross (our sins went with him). When Jesus rose from the dead, we also rose with him (cleanse from sin, made anew).

(Luke 10:19) Rom 6:14, Colo. 2:15 John 12:15, John 14:16-18

Power of the Believers' Faith

Anything we receive from God comes on the road of faith. It is not what you see with your natural eyes, but what God said in his word (James 2:19; James 1:2-4), and you believing it in your heart. You surrender all the benefits of not being faithful and obedient to God's word.

Also read: Rom 10:9-10; 1 Cor. 3:1

"What you confess with your mouth comes from your heart. It is what you say and what you do. Remember faith without works is dead."

James 1:22-23,	John 15:7
2 Peter 1:3 2,	Cor. 5:17
Gal 5:22-23,	James 1:23

You must go back to the basic instructions to take back what the devil has taken from you. Remember the seeds of tomorrow are in our children of today. We must plant the correct seeds in them, namely the word of God. It is not your fault for what Adam did, but it is your time to make it right.

Faith comes in four ways:

1. Hearing the word of God.
2. Believing in the heart.
3. Speaking with your mouth.
4. Taking action on what you believe (action is works).

The Resurrection

Because of the death and Resurrection, you have the power to do what God wants you to do. Your problem is being disobedient; you think you know more than the one who created you. We cannot have doubt; with doubt we will not accomplish anything in life. Your disobedience and unbelief stops the movement of God in your life. Only faith activates the word of God.

"Nothing is too hard for God" (Rom 10:8-9). We must have faith and believe the word of God. His death freed you of all our pain and suffering from Satan. You will be successful in all you do. If you put God first, you will never be last in anything you do.

1 Cor. 5

As I stated in the above chapter, when Jesus died on the cross, you also died on that cross. When he went to hell, you also went. When he was raised, you were raised as well. Why? Because your identity is in him; you have the power to conquer the trials and temptation of life. The Father said he would send another comforter. Which is the Holy Spirit.

You have the power to activate the spirit. Your spirit identity is greater than your worldly identity. Do you know who you are, or do you know whose you are? The church has gotten off track. The pulpit has gotten weak; it is conforming to the things of the world. Instead of accepting God, you are accepting the gold (money) and popularity. You are putting these things ahead of the word of God. All because you don't know who you are in Christ. He has given you the power to overcome those things the devil is putting in front of you. You are falling for his lies and deceit. I challenge you to really find out about your identity, your spiritual identity.

Please read Hosea 4:6, also 2 Peter 1:5-10, this all comes down to building a relationship with your Lord and savior.

"Who me?" Yes you.

> "Brethren, I count not myself to have appre-
> hended; but this one thing I do, forgetting
> those things which are behind, and reaching
> forth unto those things which are before"
> (Phil 3:13).

As parents you must be like a tree planted by the water. The water in your life is you drinking the word of God daily, when you plant yourself in the word you water your spirit and growth, you will prosper in all you do. That means raising Godly children (Psalms 1:3). When you do what the word tells you to, you don't have to blame others for what you did not do.

You have power over the devil because you are part of your Lord and savior nature. Why? Because you were created in is image (Rom 10:9,10). You must speak it. You need to know who you are in Christ (John 17:21; Colossians. 3:1-3; Eph. 2:6-8).

We share the resurrection! He died and went to hell for your sins. He defeated the devil (Read the following: Colo 2:15, Rom 6, Galatians 2:20/ Colossians 2:13). "Trust in the Lord with all thine heart; and lean not unto thine own understanding. In all thy ways acknowledge him, and he shall direct thy paths" (Proverbs 3:5,6).

Trust in the Lord with all your heart.

"I will never leave you, never forsake you" (Heb. 13:5).

We must fear (give reverence) God. Read the story of Lazarus and the rich men. We must believe the word of God. He paid the price that we should have paid. He went to hell for you. Therefore, I say every day is a good day, because Jesus went to hell for you. If you continue where you are going, being disobedient to His word, being led by social media and false teachings and blaming everyone for your disobedience, there is nothing that happens to you that you don't have a say in. You must learn when and how to say it. You were blessed to have children and given the responsibility to raise them up in the way they should go. Nowhere in the word does it say your children are your best friend. You are responsible for your children, so stop being their best friend. Love them, teach them and stop blaming everyone else for what you did not do. Being a parent is a privilege and a gift from God.

(Heb. 9:14) (Heb. 9:6)
(Heb. 10:12/1 Tim 4:2/Act 23:1)

You are believing everything you hear on social media, talk radio and TV. Don't let people put their guilt on you, do what his word tells you to do, and he will take care of the rest. (II peter 1:4) (Ez. 6:36) (II Cor 5:21) (Rom 4:25)

(Colo.1:15) (Psalms 6) (II Cor. 2:14)
(Heb. 1:3) (Cor. 3:11)

It doesn't matter what your color is, it doesn't matter your job status, but what really matters, is who you are in Jesus Christ. With Him in your life, He will direct your path.

God's grace has accomplished for more you than you could ever think of or do. Remember it is your identity in Jesus Christ, not man (II Cor. 2:14). In him, we are victorious when we acknowledge this. We will not let the devil control our thoughts or actions.

You were made in the image of God. That means you are a direct image of God. But when Adam fell, everything changed. He gave our control to the devil. Then God sent his son Jesus to redeem us to let us know our identity is in Jesus (Colo. 3:5-8).

Speaking in other tongues

"The blood of Jesus cleanses us." (Act 2:1-4; John 20:22; II Cor. 4:18; John 14:16-18)

We are to live in the supernatural because the Holy Spirit is supernatural (Deut. 26:2-10; Ezek. 44:30).

When you do what he asks you to do, he will do what he promise he would do (Prov. 28:1). In these days, we need to be bold. If we are not bold in the word of God, we would not receive the promises of God. The secret of boldness is obedient to God's word (Deut. 1:36; Eph. 3:12; I John 4:4).

Being bold is having courage, and your praise is the weapon of offence. You should never stop praising the Lord. You must learn to be a person of praise.

Praise open God's power (Chr. 20:17). Praise shuts down the devil's operation. Praise is a tool of destruction for the devil's tactics. If you have a problem or are going through some things, begin praising the lord. You. "Who me?" Yes you. Your fire has gone out and you need to get that fire back. If you never had your fire lit, it is time you get it lit. The fire I am speaking about is the burning desire to praise the Lord, to be obedient to the word of God.

When you give a shout to the Lord, things happen. "The wall came down when they shouted. Judah shouted it came to pass that God smote Jeroboam. God will only act on your word, he said we have not because we ask not" (Joshua 6:10).

Miracles come to people who need one. Miracles come to people who are wanted. We are born of God, and God is a God of miracles (I John 5:40). We need miracles for the things that are happening. We need to stop dumbing things down, drinking the Kool-Aid. The word of God. The closer you get to Jesus, the stronger your faith. The farther you are from Jesus, the more doubtful and weak you are of his word.

Mark 4 (Mark 5 healing)

The devil has no power over men and women of God. There is a big difference between just going to church so you can say you went to church today versus going to praise God and learn His word. Stop being a weekend pure sitter and going to receive something from God. You must be like the lady with the issue of blood for 12 years. She went to see Him knowing something was going to happen. You can read about it in the following scriptures: Matthew

9:20, Mark 5:25 and Luke 8:23. You must have this kind of faith in the word of God, and you will see your life change.

James 4, Mark 1:16

A form of Godliness that doesn't have God has no power.

Making the best of a trial

1. The benefit of a trial. (I Peter 1:3-7, 4:12-13) (John 14:1) (Luke 22:31) (Rev. 14:12) (Heb. 6:11) (Matt 27:3-5) (Matt 26) (I Cor. 15:45) (I Cor. 15:58) Your trial will test your loyalty to Jesus and your faith in God. The trial is for your faith. Have the spirit and nature of God. (I Gal 5:22-23)
2. Affection for others (Love)
3. Exuberance about life (Joy)
4. Serenity (peace)
5. Willingness to stick with things (Patience)
6. Compassion (kindness)
7. Basic holiness (goodness)
8. Loyalty (faithfulness)
9. Not needing to force our energies wisely (Gentleness)

10. Marshalling and directing our energies wisely (self-control) (Cols. 2:6-7-8) (Heb. 13:14)

We need to praise God more and more (Psalms 67:3-6; Rom 4; Psalms 107:31). You can get above your circumstance by praising the Lord (II Cor. 20:21-220; Psalms 149:5-8; Acts 160; Psalms 3:3).

The flesh is lazy, so we need to put down the flesh and begin to praise. We need to be known as a people of praise. If you are a praiser, then you are a positive person. Praise is the increase, praise destroys the weak of the enemy.

Chase that brings transformation. (I Cor. 1:18) (Rom 1:26) (Rom 8:8) (Roman 12:12) (Rom 8:7-9)

God gives us the power of choices. Your identity is in Christ. Your habits are what you choose. Our hang-ups and pride does not make us who we are. The world would have you to conform to its own will instead of God's will.

Living in darkness, watering down then out of darkness. The choice you make down here will determine your future, Heaven or Hell. (Rom 1:21) (James 4:4) (mark 8:34-35)

1. Focus on God's power and not your power.
2. Focus on good things and not bad things.
3. Focus on walking by faith and in what God says.

4. Focus on who is helping you.
5. Focus on being careful of being complacent. Be comprehensive. Be aware of pride.

If you don't like the game you are in, seek my Lord and savior Jesus Christ. He is a game changer.

Praise & Power

With my mouth I will bless the Lord. (Col 6:7; Psalms 35; I peter 2; Heb. 13:15)

The fruit of our life is hailing, praising the lord, but your actions are much different. (Psalms 67)

If we praise the Lord we will be blessed, but our praise must increase. Because there is power in praise (Psalms 107:31), you can't complain and praise God. The health problem is depression. If you are depressed, you are not a praiser (Rom. 4; Jonah 2:7-9; Luke 24:53; Act 2:47; Act 3:8). Praise power will lift depression off you. Believers should never be depressed (Psalms 50:230; Acts 16; Psalms 113:3; Psalms 32:11; Eph. 5:22-25).

We need to be people of praise. Then you will see the move of God like you have never seen before. Praise is power!!

The Power of Yes

Where the spirit of the Lord is, there is liberty. (Psalms 107:20)

The word travels, and human works can't override the Holy Ghost promotion (Isaiah 55; Matt 8; Jer. 33:3). If God gives you instruction (Jer. 29:11), follow them. So many people are so busy doing nothing. They can't see or understand the instruction. Now you are blaming everyone else because you say you don't have time or some other excuse not to accept that you are the reason things happen to you.

Three things of faith and obedience that will push you into your blessings:

1. You must say yes to God and no to the devil, resist the devil and he will flee. (Daniel 11:3-20)
2. You have divine protection (yes) (Prov. 28:1 30:3)1 (Rev. 5:5)
3. You will receive supernatural provision (Abraham) How to keep your miracles?

(Matt 8, Matt 17:14-20, John 14:13, John 14:14, I Cor. 12:28, I Cor. 8-10, Heb. 4:4)

People are in reasoning mode and not in the spirit. When you are in a reasoning mode, you're blocking the spirit from moving in your life (II Cor. 6:16; Heb. 13; Matt 8; Isaiah 53:4).

Divine healing comes through your human spirit. God only heals through faith and it must come from the heart (Psalms 107:20, Matt 26, James 4:7).

Also read: Matt 5:6, Neh. 8, Jer. 15:16, gen 21;1-7, Psalms 1:27, Psalms 1:2, Psalms 126, II Cor. 6, I Cor. 3:8

Without the presence of God, we have nothing. If you don't know where you are, you will never know when you get there. Your labor determines your reward. The devil must know who you are as a child of God. We must use the power that the Lord has given us. As you grew in the Lord, things the devil tried to put on you now have no power over you. When you shut down praise, you stop production, and the devil comes right back in and takes control of your thoughts and life, creating confusion. There is no self-control in the world today, no standard. We need to put the armor of God back on; if you never had it on, then you need to put it on. "The vision stays on course" (Habakkuk 2:1).

Also read: Heb. 10:35; Isaiah 6

Celebrate Recovery

Exodus 16:1-5

There are many people who have many addictions and are walking in darkness. To break through the darkness, we need Jesus, who is the light. In man's eyes it is not easy to overcome. But putting your trust in Jesus, trusting in his word helps bring us out of the darkness. What we do matters, but most of all is how we do it. He will defend us if we are being the salt and light God commanded us to be.

The anti-Christ wants you to see only what will make you think there are more people that believe what they are doing is right. I am telling you that there is a greater system (I John 1:1-6) than the system of the anti-Christ. That system is the powerful system of the Holy Spirit. The media is giving the devil power he doesn't have. Because the word tells us that "all power belongs to me said the Lord." The only power the devil has is what we give to him (John 8:32).

Holding on to Your Miracle (James 1:5)

Every day is a contest. The Devil is always trying to strip you of your blessings. We need to always be on our guard. Doubt is the enemy of faith. Doubt is unhealthy, it is a sign of weakness. Doubt is far from Jesus. Faith is close to Jesus (Matt 14:22).

When you stop acting out the word, doubt will start setting in. Doubt will take away God's best for you (Mark 6:5).

If you are fighting for your life, get around people of faith. Do not get around people of doubt. Read Mark 11:23, Matt 8:17.

Boldness

(Prov. 1) (II Tim 1:7) (Act 4:16) (Eph. 3:12) (Isaiah 4:4) (Heb. 10:19) (Heb. 13:5) (Exodus 14:14) (Luke 10:19)

I John 3, Rom 12:1-2, Deut. 28:8, Gal 5:22-23

Everything we do is a seed. Therefore, we must be careful at what we say and do. As a Christian, we are an open book. We are being watched, so we must set a holy example that people will know we are children of the highest. Remember the principle of life is seedtime and harvest (Hug 2:19, Numbers 23:24).

We live in a time of cause and effect. What we do will create the destined effect. Believe the effects of your actions.

The End Time (Revelations)

Read II Pet 1-14-21; Matt 24:42-44; Revel 22; I Cor. 15:51; Ez. 38-39; Zech. 14:1-5-12-14:14; Rev 14:20; Rev 19:11; Isaiah 13:10; Rev 20:2.

In Isaiah 65:20, at the end there is a resurrection of the dead. They will be placed in the lake of fire (Rev 21:1-27/ Rev 22:1- II Peter 10).

Psalms 73:11

Four things God doesn't know:

1. Does not know a sin, he does not hate. If you keep holding on to sin you are setting yourself up for judgement in heaven (Prov. 13:18; James 1:15)
2. God does not know a sinner that he does not love.

3. God does not know of a salvation other than John 14.
4. God II Cor. 6:2

Love is the Greatest Motivation

I John 3:16, I John 4:10, Eph. 4:16

II Cor. 5:14, mark 12:30-31, Rom 12:6&9, Gal 6:3.

The love of God is the greatest motivation you will ever have. It gives you power, strength and courage to do his will. We were created so the love of God can flow through us. We are not being selfish, but to care about others spreading the love of God to all.

Healing (Matt 8:16,17)

You must beware of the devil's tactics, as he will put sickness and pain in your body. You may be asking how can he do that, so please close attention to what I am about tell you. He brings sickness and pain upon you through your thoughts in the spirit realm, creating doubt and dis-obedience. The doubt is doubting God's word, and the dis-obedience is not following instructions. You eat and drink things that you should not, you take risks you should not. All because of the thoughts that are placed in your mind. Remember, if it is wrong, it is not of God. If something is causing you to be sick or in pain, it is not of God. You lay around not being active, you drive everywhere, even ride around the parking lot one or two times just to try and find a parking space close to the door. Stop blaming others for what you don't do for yourself. When the devil controls your thoughts, you allow him to create barriers, so you are not able to do the work of the ministry. It is God's will for you to be healed. So, stop blaming others for your sickness, you have control of your life. God gave you control over your life when He sent His only son to die for you. What you really need is Jesus. This is the only way things will change in your life. And remember it is not just what you say, but also what you do.

Isa. 5:13

Pro. 23:19

Luke 12:8-10

Act 10:38

Luke 1:9

Matt 12:15

Mark 9:12

Matt 4:23

How to keep what God gives you (II King 4:8)

Eph. 4

If you want to keep what God gives you, you need to walk in love as God told you. When we stop loving each other, we begin to lose the power of God (Matt 18:1, 18-James 1:3). There is a season of rest, and we must know when that season is. This time is to refresh and continue to pray, having faith in His word and give thanks daily.

Doubting heart

A doubting heart is more than an uncertain heart. An uncertain heart seeks direction, but a doubting heart rejects the direction it has received. To doubt is to call into question what one has received. When applied to our spiritual journeys, the heart demonstrates reluctance to follow the path God has revealed. As men, women, believers, non-believers, parents and children, you must know what the Bible says about the heart. When you take a stand for the commands you were given, there will be no doubt. You can't follow the word of God with doubt and be an overcomer. You must live and act the word by faith, remembering the issues of life start in the heart (Matt 12:34).

If you have doubts about God's word, you may want to apply the following. Remember, the cure for doubt depends to some extent on the thing doubted. However, the real problem is not in the object doubted, but in the subject who doubts. Therefore, the following steps should and can be taken by the doubting person.

1. **Confess** the doubt to God as a sin. Doubt is basically unbelief in God and His word, and it is therefore sin. God has promised to hear our confession of even the darkest unbelief (Roman 14:23, Hebrew 11:6).

2. **Study** the evidence for the Christian faith. Christians have nothing to fear by looking into the facts from any source of knowledge. The greatest evidence for the validity of Christianity, the resurrection of

Christ, is attested by much proof. Among these are the empty tomb, post-resurrection appearance and transformed disciples. Since the resurrection is true, it verifies everything the Bible says (II Timothy 2:15).

3. **Make certain of your salvation.** Paul exhorts Christians to examine themselves to make sure they are Christians (II Corinthians 13:5). Also, in the book of Hebrew 6: 1-9, salvation from sin is by simple trust in Jesus Christ. Until you are assured of your salvation, you will be troubled by enormous doubts.

4. **Faithfully study the word of God.** Faith comes by hearing, and hearing by the word (Romans 10:17). Through study and application of the Bible, our faith is strengthened and matured. Most especially, you must master the doctrine or basic teachings of the Bible if you are to be stable, mature Christians (1 Tim 4:13, II Tim 3:16, Titus 2:1-10).

5. **Pray.** The is surest way to face doubts when they come is to have an extensive history of answers prayers. The more you as a Christian pray with faith, the more you as a Christian see God answer prayers. The more you see God answer prayers, the

stronger your faith becomes and the weaker the doubt becomes.

"Get wisdom! Get understanding! Do not forget, nor turn away from the word of my mouth" (Proverbs 4:5 NKJV).

The items below are just 30 things YOU must do. I did not come up with this list, but I don't know the author of it. I just modified it to make it more personal, as I believe it can be of great help to you, my readers.

1. I (you) must be fishers of men when I (you) catch them, He will clean them.
2. A (your) family altar can alter a family. Prayer and fellowship time is the key.
3. When you do a lot of kneeling it will keep you in good standing.
4. You must stop putting a question mark where God put a full stop. Do this and you will not fall off the cliff.
5. You got to stop waiting for six strong men to take you to church. Remember His word tells us not to "not forsake the assembling of ourselves

together, as the manner of some is; but exhorting one another: and so much the more, as ye see the day approaching" (Hebrew 10:25 KJV).

6. You must get into an exercise program that is daily. The perfect partner is our Lord and Savior Jesus Christ. Walk with Him daily and you will see the difference in your mental and physical abilities.

7. Forbidden fruits create many jams.

8. Give God what's right and not what's left

9. Give Satan an inch and he will become a ruler.

10. God doesn't call the qualified, He qualifies the called.

11. God grades from the cross not on a curve, walk straight.

12. God loves everyone but, prefers fruits of the spirit over "religious nuts"!

13. God promises a safe landing not a safe passage (fight the good fight).

14. Do you have truth decay? Brush up on your Bible!

15. Remember he who angers you controls you!

16. If you are good at making excuses, you are not good anything else.

17. When you kneel (prayer) before God you can stand before anything or man!

18. Remember, kindness is very difficult to give away, because it keeps coming back.

19. Most people want to serve God, but only in their own way.

20. Never give the devil a ride! He will always want to drive.

21. Nothing ruins the truth like stretching it.

22. Plan. It wasn't raining when Noah built the ark.

23. "Pray" is a four-letter word that you can do anywhere.

24. Prayer: Don't give God instructions – just report for duty!

25. The will of God never take you to where the grace of God will not protect you.

26. If you are almost saved, you are totally lost.

27. Warning: If you are exposed to the Son, it may prevent burning!

28. You need to watch your step, because everyone else is watching.

29. You should not change God's message, but let the message change you.

30. When you start to worry you enter the darkroom where doubt and negatives are developed.

Remember, you are the one that control your destination, so stop blaming others for what you have control of.

Chapter 9

MONEY

We need it to survive in this world today, but somehow everything we do involves money. We can't get around not using it. Our problem is not having money, but the money having us. We steal it, we borrow it, we loan it, we spend it, we donate it, we loan it to others, etc. When we do these things with it, we don't seem to have a problem. But when it comes to giving to the house of God to help build the Kingdom here and abroad, paying our tithes or giving offerings, we complain.

We moan about it, we complain to others we even leave the church. If the pastor talks about money, the non-believers, non-givers are the ones that are always being negative about giving. We as believers know the word of God is free. But getting it to you costs money. Things like having a place to have service, rent/mortgage, lights and water, recordings and maintenance are just a few things that must be paid for. We are the church, you are the church, you were given the task to take the gospel to the world (Mark 16:15). Now how will we do that? This can only be done by having what?

You also have the responsibility to help the community. How can we do that if we don't have money? Here is what Genesis 8:22 tells you: "While the earth remaineth, seedtime and harvest, and cold and heat, and summer and winter, and day and night shall not cease."

This is telling you whatever you plant (sow) there will come a time when you will have a harvest on what you plant. If you don't plant anything, you will not have anything to harvest. Let me put it another way. You have a bank account when you make deposits. You know you can go back and make withdraws. On the flip side, if you did not put anything in your account, then you don't have anything to take out of your account. Now, here is the good thing about sowing. You will reap what you sow, you are helping to bless someone somewhere and you are being obedient to the word of God. When you are in need, you can now make withdrawals from your account because you made deposits. The bank teller in this case is our Lord and Savior Jesus Christ. Here are a few things you can withdraw from your account. There are three parts to sowing:

1. Prayer, you must pray always.
2. Fasting (there are some things you must pray and fast for).
3. Faith (faith without works is dead).

We must always try to live a balanced life of spirit, mind and body.

Healing, job, promotion and pay increase are just a few things you can get when you have faith and obedience to the word of God

You. "Who me?" Yes you.

I know there are many pastors and preachers who have taken advantage of the church. Stealing, embezzling money you gave to God. I tell you God will take care of them. You must be obedient to his word and do your part. Remember, the church, is the people (you). We are to watch and pray and not let things like embezzlement take place in the church. Money is one of the biggest things that separates you from God and others. Relationships are broken apart because of a lack of money or even having too much money. All because you fell in love with money.

When you are blessed to have more than someone else, you are to help someone that is in need. But some of us don't, not realizing you did not get the money by yourself. Someone gave it to you! Someone purchased something from you or you provided a service for it. This is what the word is telling you. "For the love of money is the root of all evil: which while some coveted after, they have erred from the faith, and pierced themselves through with many sorrows" (1 Timothy 6:10). Look around and you will see all the evil that is happening because of the love of money.

Money is something you can't take with you when you die.

You are in your situation because of you and no one else. You made the choices that put you where you are. Yes, you had help getting there, but as we all know God did not create us to be alone. The problem comes when we think we have made it and we don't need people or God anymore. This also includes individuals claiming to be Christians. Once you think you have made it, you change your walk, you change the way you talk, you change who you hang out with. You start purchasing your toys, forgetting about your obedience to the word of God. You put yourself first, and the things of God are slowly moving to the back of the line. The money begins to take control of you and now no one can tell you anything. You think you are above everyone else.

This is what the word of God tells us. "For the love of money is root of all evil: which while some coveted after, they have erred from the faith, and pierced themselves through with many sorrows" (1 Timothy 6:10). I said all to this to tell you don't let money control you. Follow the word of God and be obedient to His word. Remember, money is very important in the kingdom of God, but you must be in control, not the money controlling you. His word tells you to give, and "it shall be given unto you; good measure, pressed down, and shaken together, and running over, shall men give into you bosom. For with the same measure that ye mete withal it shall be measure to you again" (Luke 6:38). It is a blessing to have money, and God wants all to be prosperous.

III John 1:2 tells us "Beloved, I wish above all things that thou (you) mayest prosper and be in health, even as thy soul prospereth." He is not against you having; it is the sharing you are not doing. In the book of Malachi 3:8, God asks this question: "Will a man rob God? Yet ye have robbed me. But ye say, wherein have we robbed thee? In tithes and offerings." When we bless the Kingdom of God, He will bless us in many ways, in ways we can't imagine. On the other hand, when you are selfish, you will have only what you have. I believe you get blessed so you can bless others. This don't have to always be with money. It could be with friendship, love or compassion. These are just a few things people are also in need of. The reason I am writing about money is to remind you of what the word says about it. Also, the word of God is free, but it takes money to get the word to the people. If we are to do what it says in Mark 16:15, we need money. If you were obedient to His word, we wouldn't have the problems we have today getting the word to the people. The last thing I will say to you about money is, "Who me?" Yes you.

About money in the kingdom of God, remember to read the following scriptures. "For what shall it profit a man, if he shall gain the whole world, and lose his own soul?" (Mark 8:38).

Your money and the things you get with it is causing you to put God second in your life, and you are asking yourself how does he know this. It is your action that speaks for you. "And thou say in thine heart, my power and the might of mine hand hath gotten this wealth" (Deuteronomy

8:17). When you put God last, you have no one to blame except yourself.

"Who me?" Yes you.

"But thou shall remember the Lord thy God: for it is he that giveth thee power to get wealth, that he may establish his covenant which he sware unto thy father, as it is this day" (Deuteronomy 8:18).

I believe you are given this power so that you can help further the Kingdom of God. You can't take what you have been given with you when you die, so with that being said, help others by planting seeds of giving, and that will last forever. "Give, and it shall be given unto you; good measure, pressed down, and shaken together, and running over, shall men give into your bosom for with the same measure that ye mete withal it shall be measure to you again" (Luke 6:38). This is telling you whatever you give it will be given back to you. If you give a little you will receive little, if you give much you will receive much.

**Note What you have can be taken/lost in the blink of an eye. God gives you the power to get wealth. You need put the kingdom first, and giving is part of the promises of the Kingdom.

When you are obedient, you will see the promise. Faith, when acted on, will show you God's work. When you show love and compassion to others, these are the keys open the door to God's Kingdom.

Chapter 10

"WHO ME?" YES YOU

If you want to know who can solve the problems of the world today? I would tell you to look in the mirror.

"Who me?" Yes you.

Remember God created man for his pleasure and gave you dominion in this earth. But something happened in the garden of Eden. Adam and Eve sold out to a lie of the devil, creating sin through disobedience. One man sold you out, but another man bought you back. His name is Jesus, God sent his only son to die for you. He took all your sins, sicknesses and diseases on that cross. He gave you back what the devil stole, he has given you back the power to control your destiny. So, stop blaming everyone for what you do or don't do.

The following are a few nuggets I picked up in reading and in listening to preachers, teachers and the spirit. You may want to put them in your shopping cart. The following four things can prevent you from being a team player, so be mindful about getting caught up in them.

1. **Gossip**: Always speaking and listening to negative things about others.
2. **Pride**: You will not say you are sorry when you are wrong. Not asking for forgiveness.
3. **Envy**: You are jealous of what someone else have.
4. **Disobedient**: You are not following God's instructions,

The following things will make you a team player:

1. **Obedient**: Following the game plan the coach has laid out for the game.
2. **Support**: (Stand up for the team in fight to accomplishing the goal.
3. **Encouragement**: Help teammates when things are not going well lift them up.
4. **Studying**: Reviewing the play book daily memorize the plays.
5. **Praying for team mates**: This you must do every day. We are to always pray.

Seven things you do that stop you in your efforts in life:

1. **You** have no clear written goal in mind.
2. **You** have no clear metrics to measure your progress.
3. **You** believe more information is better before getting started.
4. **You** believe fitness doesn't matter.
5. **You** believe you aren't meant to have good things.
6. **You** believe bigger is better.
7. **You** have to much pride to get help.

We must live like children of the King. Here are 10 things you can put in your shopping cart.

1. **You** can live like heaven is on earth.
2. **You** must love like you have never been hurt.
3. **You** must play like you already won.
4. **You** can dream the sky is the limit.
5. **You** must give like there is no tomorrow.
6. **You** must sing for joy like no one can hear you.
7. **You** must dance like no one is watching.
8. **You** must smile until it hurts.

9. **You** must laugh like no one is listening.
10. **You** must cherish your family and friends until death.

Everything that happens to you is because of you.

"Who me?" Yes you!!

We never look at the part we play or did not play to create the situation we are in. The word of God tells us we have a choice. If you have a choice, why are you blaming others? Joshua 24:15 tells us to choose you this day whom we will serve.

Chapter 11

SOCIAL MEDIA/NEWS

All news is not bad news, but you got to know what is true and what false. There are very few positive stories reported. You have created a two-headed monster, as everything you see around you was created by you. So, if you don't like what you see, blame the person you see in the mirror. As my pastor would say, don't drink the Kool-Aid, which is what the news and social media is serving. If you keep drinking the poison, you will end up like the people that followed Jim Jones in the 80's, known as the Tragedy in Guyana. When you look and listen to what is happening around you, can you see something is happening that is not of God. Children young and old are losing their minds, killing each other, all because of a lack of knowledge and the rejection of knowledge (Hosea 4:6).

God has done His part. He created you in His image. He sent His only son to die for you. All He asks is for you to be obedient to His word and stop blaming others for what you do or did not do. You are in a spiritual battle, and if you are not using what you have been given, you are drinking the Kool-Aid, losing this battle to a devil that has been defeated by our Lord and Savior Jesus Christ. This is what Matthew 4:4 tells us, "But he answered, it is written, Man does not live by bread alone, but by every word that comes from the mouth of God." Yes, I know you are not perfect, and God is not looking for perfect people. He is looking for obedience from His children, who know how to ask for forgiveness and repent when they do wrong.

There is so much distraction in the world today, created in the minds of man. Everyone that is mentally weak in their mind will fall for the things of the world, the lies, deceit and glamor. They will have you thinking and saying, "Well, I am only human, I can make a mistake." Yes, you can, but doing it repeatedly is not a mistake. You have moved from a mistake to intentional, and this where you created your destination. We should not give place to the devil; therefore, it is so important to stay in the word daily. Yes, you will be tempted, but this is what the word says.

"There hath no temptation taken you, but such
as is common to man: but God is faithful,

who will not suffer you to be tempted above
that ye are able; but will with the temptation
also make a way to escape, that ye may be
able to bear it."

There is no excuse for your action or inaction for the
situation you are in. Remember, you create your own situation—no one else. You have no one to blame but you.
Here is one way we get into situations you think you can't
get out of. You see something you admire, and once you
start admiring it, you move to desiring it, then you move to
acquiring it. In many cases, it is something you don't need
or something that belongs to someone else. This is how
the devil works in the spirit world. Your spirit mind is very
important; you must build it through the word of God. You
must read the word daily, you must always pray to build
you spirit up in the word of God. The devil works on the
weak, so if you are one that goes to bed with social media
and wakes up with your social media, you are a prime
target for the influence of the devil's tactics. We know
social media can be a good thing when using it in a positive way. We know when something is created for good,
the devil turns it into evil. You are the one in control, not
the devil, so stop drinking the lies and negative Kool-Aid

that is being served on Facebook, Instagram, LinkedIn and any other social media that is out there. Remember, when you put God first, you will not be last in anything you do.

Chapter 12

YOU

You are God's creation and by being His creation you are the center of everything. When you are the star everyone wants a piece of you. Therefore, it is so Important for you to know the word of God. This is what his word tells you, Study to show thyself approved unto God, a workman that needed not to be ashamed, rightly dividing the word truth (II Timothy 2:15). Here is one of the main reasons to study the word. You must beware of false prophets, which come to you in sheep's clothing, but inwardly they are ravening wolves (Matt.7:15). With everything social media, the news and the water down word that is coming from some pull pits around the world. You must know how to divide the word, if you want to receive the promise you must live the word.

Remember, you are the center of attraction. Nothing is done without you; you create your own environment. You do this by what you say and do, and all of it comes from what you see and hear. In life, things are placed in front of you. They can be either good or evil, which is in the spirit realm. The stronger of the two will always win, which is another reason for you to study and know the word. The five D's of the devil described above are just some of the devil's tactics. You are confronted with these daily. How you deal with them is the key to life or death.

I ask you to look inside yourself and ask yourself, have I let these things slip into my though pattern, creating negative vibes and blaming others for what I control and did not do anything or went too far?

I believe the only way you cannot fall for the devil's devices is to study the word of God and being strong in your faith of God. Remember what the word of God tells you in 1 Corinthians 10:13: "There hath no temptation taken you but such as is common to man: but God is faithful, who will not suffer you to be tempted above that ye are able; but will with temptation also make a way to escape, that ye may be able to bear it."

So, there is no excuse for you not getting out of your situation when you have faith in God's word. Use the faith you have been given to maintain the victory over the devil, and remember if God's word said it, believe it (Roman 12:3).

Note: You must be aware of whom and what you are dealing with in high places. **This is another reason why you should follow what God has laid out in His word.**

Live by the 3 C's of Life: Choice, chance and change.

You must make a _____ to take a _____
to make a _____ . What will you do?
Write some thoughts here: _____

_____

_____

_____

The bottom line is that you need to take God out of the box. Yes, you have Him in a box and you only want to use Him when you want something from Him. Then you open the box and want to make withdrawals, but did you put anything in the account to get something out? You have not read the word, you don't pray, you are not tither, always speaking negative about the pastor and the operation of the church. Some of you don't have Him in a box, you have Him at the bottom of your list of things. You may be asking "What list?" Well, I am glad you asked that. The list I'm talking about consists of the following. These are just a few items on your long list.

1. Money
2. Social Media
3. Cell Phone
4. Computer
5. Television
6. New Car
7. God

These are just a few things you put ahead of God. There are other things you know you are doing that you and only God know. Re-adjust your list and you will see the change. When you put God first, you will never be last in anything. His word says He will never leave you nor forsake you (Hebrews 13:5). "If ye abide in me, and my word abide in you, ye shall ask what ye will, and it shall be done unto you" (John 15:7).

You can't put the creator in a box or put him on the bottom of your list and expect to receive from Him. He must be first in all our lives. Faith is the key to the activation of God's promises. Because you don't have faith in His word, you are the one that is stopping your blessings. Stop blaming others for your lack of knowledge and start reading His word. Your lack of knowledge is allowing the devil's thoughts to enter, creating doubt about God's word. When doubt enters, in come sickness, depression, deceit, lies, blinded eyes and the blame game because you don't see your part in what is happening around you. This can easily happen when the devil has you in darkness. We can overcome all of this if we apply the following three things:

1. Obedience (doing what you have been or are told to do by His word)
2. Faith (in what His word says)
3. Love (you must love one another)

You live and die by what you say, and you are the real reason things happen to you. The word of God says let a man examine himself. If you want to see a change in what you say and do, you must make that decision—no one else. Stop blaming others for what you control. Ask God to create in you a clean ___. "O God; and renew a right_ within me" (Psalms 51:10). When you ask this, it must be in faith, and you follow up with action.

I pray this book has opened your eyes to how important you are and the power you have to make a difference in this world. Below are a few scriptures for the New Birth. If you have not accepted Jesus Christ as your Lord and Savior, now is a good time to except Him.

Do you believe Jesus died for you, and that the Father God raised him from the dead?

Are you willing to confess that Jesus is now your Lord?

Then go ahead and say it: Jesus is now my Lord.

You have now declared that you believe Jesus is now your Lord. You have said with your mouth that Jesus is now your Lord, now go and live like Jesus is now your Lord.

Read the following scriptures:

Romans 10:9, (King James Version) Roman 5:12, (KJV)

John 1:12, (KJV)

John 3: 16, (KJV)

Ephesians 2:8, (KJV)

CPSIA information can be obtained
at www.ICGtesting.com
Printed in the USA
FFHW011356170519
52522056-57958FF